T0077429

MY *Dwelling* PLACE

MARGARET GREENE

WestBow
PRESS
A DIVISION OF THOMAS NELSON

WestBow Press books may be ordered through booksellers or by contacting:

WestBow Press
A Division of Thomas Nelson
1663 Liberty Drive
Bloomington, IN 47403
www.westbowpress.com
1-(866) 928-1240

ISBN: 978-1-4497-2076-6 (sc)

Library of Congress Control Number: 2012923009

Printed in the United States of America

WestBow Press rev. date: 12/07/2012

This book is dedicated to:

My four wonderful children,
Samuel, Monnie, Johnathan and Nathalie
Thank you for following the teaching of
living a life Holy in the sight of God

In loving memory of,
My deceased mother, father, step-father, sisters and brothers
Ruth Johnson, Nathaniel Johnson, Joe Cochran,
Mamie Singleton, Carolyn Bailey,
Osborne Johnson and Timothy Johnson

All my sisters and brothers and immediate family
Douglas, Laretha, Sheila, Rhonda, and Stephanie

All my "darling grand-children"
and
My precious great-grandchild

And to all the wonderful people that
God has placed in my life

Last but not least
to
Every reader that is inspired by reading this book

INTRODUCTION

My Dwelling Place is the story of my trials that I have encountered in life, but the glorious part is that I have not been defeated and I found my dwelling place and rested in Him. I do not want you to concentrate on the trials but look at the triumphs. The road of "following Jesus Christ is always victorious. No matter how bleak it my seem, in the valley or on the mountain top, know that God will never leave you or forsake you. Sometimes in prayer, it may be that we get a "no" answer but know that God knows what is best for us. God is sovereign, and He is working the situation out in our favor. Do not view a "no" as a denial but as a demonstration of God's divine wisdom.

I want to allow you, as the reader, to know that as Christians that we are not immune to life's trials. We must learn that it is not what we go through but how we go through it. The question I want you to ask yourself is, … Am I trusting God or relying on my own strength? "For when I am weak, then I am strong" (2 Cor. 12:10). We must totally depend on God. Wait on the Lord, no matter how long it may seem to take. The Bible tells us " Wait on the Lord: be of good courage, and He shall strengthen thine heart: wait, I say, on the Lord" (Ps. 27:14).

Whatever trial or test you are going through in life, God's grace is sufficient. Trials come to make us strong. Trials brings out God's character in us. Do not allow situations or circumstances to mobilize you to the point that you cannot see God. Hold on to the faithfulness of God. As long as you hold on to the faithfulness of God you cannot go wrong. Faith does not look at itself or at the person who is exercising it….faith looks at God. Faith is interested in God only, and it talks about God and it praises God and it extols the virtues of God. The measure of the strength of a man's faith, always, is ultimately the measure of his knowledge of God….He knows that we can rest on this knowledge. "Forever, O Lord, Your word is settled in heaven. Your faithfulness endures to all generations" (Ps. 119: 89-90).

As I pondered and prayed about "What would be the title of this book?" I was inspired while studying God's Word in Psalm 91:1 " He that dwelleth in the secret place of the most High shall abide under the shadow of the Almighty". It dropped so heavy in my spirit as I read that passage over and over that God is my dwelling place! God gave me the assurance that He was my dwelling place as I dwelled under His wings while going through every challenge in life. "Lord, thou hast been our dwelling place in all generations. Before the mountains were brought forth or ever thou had'st formed the earth and the world, even from everlasting to everlasting, thou art God" (Psalm 90:1-2). God is with us always, even before the beginning of time. God is Alpha and Omega!

I am encouraging you as you embark in the message that goes forth in this book to learn that God will equip you to face any trial that you may go through. Look to the hills, that is where your help comes from, ... God alone. "For which cause we faint not; but though our outward man perish, yet the inward man is renewed day by day. For our light affliction, which is but for a moment, worketh for us a far more exceeding and eternal weight of glory; while we look not at the things which are seen, but at the things which are not seen: for the things which are seen are temporal; but the things which are not seen is eternal" (11 Corinthians 4:16-18). It is my prayer that this book will help some to go to a "Dwelling Place", which is in the secret place of the most High…..the present help in the time of trouble.

MY DWELLING PLACE

So many of us make the statement, "I plan to do this or I plan to do that in our lives," without realizing that there must be a balance between faith and careful planning. "I" is what I want you 'not' to focus on and move… self out the way. First, we must know that we can not do anything without God's help. It is certainly good to look at future endeavors but we must never forget to apply Gods' Word to our plans. First, the wisdom of knowing that God Word says, "For I know the plans I have for you, declares the Lord, "plans to prosper you and not to harm you, plans to give you hope and a future (Jeremiah 29:11-14). Resting on the Word…Plans to prosper you, mean that you will flourish or thrive. Not to harm you…mean that even going thru the storms of live that no danger will come upon you. That assurance in itself is more than enough to rest on. We should make plans…counting on God to direct us (Proverbs 16:9) in every thing that we

5

do. We must walk by faith and place our lives in God's hands knowing that the favor we need comes from the Lord. To walk by faith does not mean that we stop planning, thinking or taking advice. All our plans must be Gods' will for our lives. Keep in mind, "whatever does not *begin* with God...will *end* in " (Proverbs 19:2) failure. "Many are the plans in a man's heart but it is the Lord's purpose that prevails.

As we plan to go through life journey, there is many hills and valleys we must encounter. Some of our trials just come from "living." We encounter physical, mental, financial and many other trials that seem to knock us for a real loop. No matter where we go, we can't escape the trial of "faith." Trying to avoid it is like changing jobs every time we have to work a little harder to get a job done. Not realizing that the next job maybe harder than the workplace you left, now you are in the same situation or maybe worst. You realize that you can't out-run God-ordained trials. There is certainly no such thing as purposeless trials. Each trial is to launch us to a new spiritual level. There is two (2) things about trials: (1) The reason for the trial, and (2) The result of the trial. The Bible tells us in James 1:2 "Consider it all joy... when you encounter various trials. We must learn to be thankful for all our trials because they give us revelation knowledge of who we are, whose we are and what remains unresolved inside our heart. Trials are keys to problems God wants us to deal with so that we will be transformed into the likeness of his Son, The Lord Jesus Christ. Trials and tribulations help produce our very character God is looking for. But know; no matter what the trial, they are not sent by God. You are never tempted by God... James 1:13.

Wherein you greatly rejoice, though now for a season, if need be, you are in heaviness through manifold temptations: That the trial of your faith, being much more precious than of gold that will perish, though it be tried with fire, might be found unto praise and honor and glory at the appearing of Jesus Christ: (Peter 1:6-7.) Our trials are red flags warning us of areas of possible danger in our lives. If we ignore them or pretend they do not exist or avoid them, they pop up some where else in our lives until we are forced to deal with them. For example: If we, that when confronted with a difficult situation, loose our patience and become angry or bitter then **it may not be the situation that God wants you to focus on but it may be your attitude about the situation that needs most of the attention.** God is just using the situation to get your attention by flashing a red light on the problem you need to resolve in your self. *Beloved, think it not strange concerning the fiery trial which is to try, though some strange thing happened unto you: But rejoice,*

inasmuch as you are partakers of Christ's sufferings; that,
when His glory shall be revealed, you may be glad also with
exceeding joy: (1 Peter 4:12-13).

I know that many, many inspirational books have been
written and will continue to be written in this lifetime,
but as I read the Word in 2 Corinthians 3:3, it really
pricked my spirit concerning writing this book. The
Word stated: " Clearly you are an epistle of Christ....
written not with ink but by the Spirit of the living God,
not on tablets of stone but on tables of flesh; that is, of
the heart." My intention is not only to write about what
is good but to surely live by example. I read once that....
One man in a thousand can write a book to instruct
others....but EVERY man can be a pattern of living
excellence to those around him. So then I asked myself
this question, "If someone were to read my life like a
book, would they find Jesus in the pages?" Many times
in conversation or just merely thinking, I have made the
statement "If I should write some of my life experiences,
I pray that it would be a blessing to someone." Not that
my life has been so different from many people, but
I realized that it is not what you go through but how
you go through it. Our life experiences are not just a
testimony for us, but a blessing for someone else. This
book was inspired to be a blessing to many. So don't lose
sight as you read on.

As I continued to embark upon writing this book these are some of the scriptures and passages that immediately came to mind that I will share with you at this time:

- When you walk through the fire, you shall not be burned....Isaiah 43:2
- In my distress I cried to the Lord, and He heard me....Psalm 120:1
- I will rember the works of the Lord; surely I will remember Your wonders of old.....Psalm 77:11
- Great triumphs are born out of great troubles.
- Difficulties in our lives give us the opportunity to experience the faithfulness of God.
- Faith never knows where it is being led, but loves and knows the One who is leading.

These are just a few of the many scriptures and passages that you can rely on to give you the added strength to walk through the trials of life.

REFLECTION

It was the summer of 1993 when it all began to unfold. I was riding in my car mediating on God's Word and reflecting back on many occurrences that had taken place in my life. Sometimes in life we must reflect back in order for us to move forward. I did not say ..."go back", I said "reflect back", which is quite different. Jesus said in Luke 9:62, "No one, having put his hand to the plow, and looking back, is fit for the kingdom of God." Just reflecting back on where God has brought us from, allow us to move forward and see how far God has brought us from. Which comes to mind at this very moment is the old hymn.....When I "think" of the goodness of Jesus and all He has done for me, my soul cries out hallelujah....I thank God for saving me. Reflecting back on some of my life experiences that day in 1993 made me realize at that very moment how bless I am to be save. I felt in my spirit to start writing things down, which resulted in me waking up three and four o'clock in the mornings to jot things down as God gave them to me and that's how this all began.

THE JOURNEY

My family and I had just relocated from Boston, Massachusetts to Atlanta, Georgia in 1993, because of the transfer of my husband job. But first, let me take you back a little before my relocating to Atlanta. I am married and have four children, three sons and one daughter. We resided in the inner city of Boston. There is lot of difficulty raising teenagers in an inner city; due to gang activities, drugs and providing a stable environment for children. In the summer of 1992 there had been many fatalities due to gang violence. Teenagers were killed constantly for such foolishness as "turf war." There was constant stress not knowing whether our children would be the next victim of such senseless killing. My husband and I prayed about leaving Boston to avoid having that tragedy happen to us. We realized that things of this nature can occur anywhere, but we knew that we simply needed a change and to better our children environment. In the midst of me wanting to leave, the thought of me leaving Boston made me have second thoughts because of the love of my church home, family, friends and my job, but I knew in my spirit that a change had to take place. We asked ourselves "If we leave where would we want to go?" We began to pray about us relocating, especially after my son best friend was murdered. Sometimes it takes tragedies to put urgency in your prayer life. Not that we can ever hurry God, but our prayers was answered immediately. "Do not be anxious about anything, but in everything, by prayer and petition, with thanksgiving, present your requests to God" (Philippians 4:6).

I am a nurse and I worked in the inner city community clinic in Roxbury, Massachusetts, which was surrounded by many gang members. It was a challenge to go to work and return home safe daily. There was many days that gun fire rang out so close to my job. So you can see why I was so compelled to make a change. I thank God for His blood covering. One day as I sat at my desk at work, a call came from my husband and he was sounding so excited and asked me to meet him for lunch. It was snowing outside and I truly did not want to encounter the cold weather. He convinced me into meeting him to share with me some good news. As I approached him I could see the happiness in his face. The first thing he said was "Honey, what have we been praying for?" I responded

"There is quite a few things that we have been praying for." and he continued to say "But what have we just asked God to do for us?" After several minutes of thinking what he was talking about, he responded, "Honey not only are we relocating but God gave us the destination of where we wanted to be! I was just astonished that God had answered our prayer that quick and so precisely. Knowing that God can answer our prayer while it is being sent up, is just a testimony of His faithfulness. So here my husband job were relocating us to Atlanta, Georgia and that prayer has been answered. We began to make preparations for a new journey. Little did we know that this was a beginning for many open chapters in our lives.

It was that final day for departure to Atlanta in July 1993. Our trials began from the very beginning of leaving Boston. Our flight were departing at 7:15PM and it was approximately 5:30PM, in rush hour, and my youngest son was no where to be found. He was the only one of our children that was leaving with us at the time; and the other three would join us later. My son was to go to the barber shop and return home, but instead he visited with all his friends. We had to search all over Boston for him and to top it off the movers still had not moved all our furniture out of our home. With prayer, coaching of the movers and rushing, we got off on time. It was still disturbing leaving the other three children behind but I knew that God's plan is perfect.

We arrived in Atlanta and stayed with my husband's sister in-law. The couple lived in Stone Mountain, Georgia, which is the suburb area of Atlanta. It was July 3rd and the weather was sweltering. The heat so intense to us because it was still jacket-wearing weather in Boston. We finally got picked up from the airport and off to Stone Mountain, Georgia we went. My husband learned that his job was very far from where they stayed and we did not have transportation at the time. We stayed there three weeks and all I can say is that was an experience. People tend to get tired real fast. We prayed earnestly that the home-finder locate us a home real fast.

It started with one disappointment after the other. I had to remind myself that God never makes a mistake. My son was very sad about leaving and he was certainly missing the other children and his friends. I felt lonely at times because my husband wasn't there because he had to report to his new job immediately. In my loneliness I prayed and realized that being alone isn't a bad thing but in times it's absolutely necessary to hear from God.

The job promised my husband a sum of money when we arrived in Atlanta, which was delayed. The furniture arrived earlier than what was scheduled and the furniture had to placed in storage. Obtaining our furniture from storage were very expensive and it placed such a hardship on our budget. The home-finder was still searching for a home close to my husband job, which she wasn't having any success at this point. My husband job was in an affluent area of Ga, so the homes was quite more expensive than we had planned to spend. We finally found a home in the Buckhead area of Georgia and was very please just to be in our own home again.

We settled in our home and started adjusting to our new environment in Atlanta. At this time my son still seemed a little out of touch at this moment because he was so shy and had problems with meeting new people. I was looking forward to him starting school and meeting new friends. It was such a chore getting him out the house because of the intense heat. School was about to begin and with much prayer, he met a neighbor that was his age and attended the same school. Just as he was settling in real good, he injured his shoulder from an accident; which resulted in him becoming really withdrawn.

But as time went on, the adjustment period did get better. A year later we moved to the Dunwoody area of Georgia and all the other children moved from Boston with us at this time. My husband nor our son was driving when we first moved to Atlanta; and both got their licenses, which made them very happy. We had a way to get around and to find a church home. I started working in my field of nursing and we were getting along well. But know; that just when you think all is going well, Satan is always on his job.

My daughter started dating a young man and became pregnant. That was a trying time for everyone at that point. The devil was fighting on every side to convince us that the move was a mistake. But in all this I knew that I had to stand on God's promises. He promised to never leave or forsake me.

In life we sometimes think that "what else could happen?" I am a living witness to tell you that trials will come. The purpose of prayer is not to get what we want, but to become what God want for us. "Pray continually; give thanks in all circumstances, for this is God's will for you in Christ Jesus" (1Thessalonians 5: 17-18).

It was many trials along the way but God brought us through them all. It was the winter of 1999 and my husband had to have emergency surgery to his left eye; which resulted in permanent lose of eyesight to that eye. As I said, that Satan's job is to kill, steal and destroy and he was trying to steal my joy. But I knew that the "Joy

being that I am a nurse, and said in my mind "that is strange for a code to be called in outpatient." At that moment I never imagined that this code was being called for my husband. The doctor came out and asked could he speak with me. I attempted to get up and my book fell open to that very same story of that women with the breast cancer. Isn't God amazing how He prepares us for situations that we are so unaware of. That same story was preparing me for what I was about to hear. The doctor said that my husband had aspirated into his lungs and they called a Pulmonary doctor in at this time. He said immediately "Let's pray" and we began to pray and then the Pulmonary doctor arrived and joined us in prayer. God takes care of His own. He surrounded my spouse with believers. I was then called to go to ICU (Intensive Care Unit) at that time because my husband was still not breathing on his own. In all the excitement I forgot to ask about the cyst; which was the main reason for him having the surgery. I turned to the doctor and said "what was the result of the biopsy?" Immediately I noticed his facial expression and he gave me the dreadful news. The biopsy was malignant. My husband had T-Cell Lymphoma, which is one of most rare and deadly form of skin cancer. I stood there speechless at that moment. I began to pray and said "I know that he is healed by Jesus stripes and God you have the final word." As I stood there in ICU just watching my husband on the breathing machine, it seemed that time stood still. I stayed there four days without leaving my husband bedside, just praying and asking God for direction.

It's easy for us to panic when we face serious concerns--a love one with cancer, the loss of a job, a wayward child. But this is the time to "stand still and wait on God." So we pray... and we get busy. We start doing everything we can to move forward in a positive way....then we worry. We know it's a waste of time to worry. Yet a lot of us find ourselves in this dilemma---we know we should trust God, but we wonder just what He's going to do. That's when we need to turn to His Word---to remind us that He is walking with us and inviting us to hand over to Him our worries and burdens. Scripture tells us, "[Cast] all your care upon Him, for He cares for you" (1 Peter 5:17), and "God shall supply all your need according to His riches in glory by Christ Jesus" (Phil. 4:19). Remember in times like these, we must learn to: "Trust in the Lord with all thine heart; and lean not unto thine own understanding. In all thy ways acknowledge Him and He shall direct thy paths" (Proverbs 3:5,6).

Months went by and my husband were receiving chemotherapy and radiation, which resulted in him returning to work. After several months he was in remission. We tend to now think about what is going to happen next or how are we going to deal with certain situations. When your mind turns to anxious thoughts about the future, remember that "your heavenly Father knows" (Matt. 6:32) and will give you what you need. My husband joined church and was being involved in many church activities. This was such a blessing for me at this time. Knowing that your husband know his rightful place in God is awesome. Blessed is the man who finds wisdom (Proverbs 3:13).

Just when you think things is going well, sometimes the bottom seem to drop out. We were faced with two (2) house fires. The house fires were two months apart. We were living in Dunwoody (the suburbs area of Atlanta) and did not think at that time to purchase fire insurance at the time. The first fire almost consumed all our belongings. We moved to another place not far from where we were before and two months later we were faced with the other fire. This time my husband got third degree burns to his face and hands. With cancer, it was a hard healing process. The doctors used various kinds of medication, but nothing seem to work. I took my "anointing oil" and applied to the burn areas and immediately we seen results. There is nothing too hard for God! Not only did the physical healing took place but the "spiritual healing" began. The doctors were amazed and stated "whatever you are doing, keep doing it". My husband faith began to grow even more. It was still trial after trial and it was a task at times to stay focus and to-- Let go and let God. Some of the trials that I encountered were the death of my four year old grandson in a car accident, my 15 year old son going to jail and tried as an adult, my middle son having a bout with depression, my two older grandchildren separated from my oldest son for five years, my daughter getting pregnant, the loss of two sisters and a two brothers, these are just a few of my many trials at this time.

I was asked many times, "How can you make it?" At times I had to wonder myself but I knew if I continued to trust God, I will make it through it all. No matter what may be the test, God will carry you through it. I know that times may be very hard but I had to trust in the Lord. We must keep in mind that the battle is not yours but it is the Lord.

Well, here comes the test of times. I'm busy at work, in the middle of a conference call, and I received a message from a co-worker that I had an important telephone call. I reminded them to hold all my calls but I could see the urgency in her demeanor that I needed to take this call. On the other end of the telephone was complete silence, then I heard crying. I kept saying hello, hello, then my husband voice appeared. He told me to come to his doctor office immediately. I discontinued my conference call and went rushing to his doctor office. Upon arrival at the doctor office, the look on his face made me realize that I wasn't getting a good report. My husband broke down sobbing immensely and stated "the cancer has come back." I took him in my arms and began praying. I told that devil that he is a liar and we are standing on the promises of God. God is a healer! At this time I felt so weak and numb, but I knew I had to be strong at this point to encourage my husband that we are going on no matter what report we received because God has the final report..

Again, we went through the process of chemotherapy, radiation therapy and numerous hospitalizations. My husband faith began to rise as he would always say---I know that God can heal me, but if He does not heal me in my physical body, I know that I am healed in my spiritual body. Sometimes, we as Christians, think that we are walking by faith and not by sight. When we have to truly stand the test of times, we see that our "faith walk" is not that easy. My husband truly demonstrated "walking by faith." That gave me such encouragement. We battled this disease for four long years. On January 20, 2004 the Lord called him home. As I sat next to his bed, a few days before he died; I asked him " Do you love me?' His reply was "I love Jesus first and then you." What a reply! I just smiled and gave him a big kiss. I knew that he had prepared himself to go on home to be with the Lord. My husband was only 48 years old at his death. I know that it is not how long we live, but how we lived. I felt so helpless, lonely and quite dispel at that moment. The scripture that kept me going at that time was---"To be absent from the body is to be present with the Lord." And to know that our greatest strength is often shown in our ability to stand still and trust God.

Grief is messy. All of us grieve at one time or another… including those of us who are Christ-followers. Many of us in the pass; who haven't experience personal loss have said to friends, "I know what you are going through." We really don't know that pain until we have personally experience it for ourselves. For the believer, however, there is something beyond the tears, pain, and loss. There is hope. As much as it hurts, we as Christians knows…. because Christ lives, death is not tragedy but triumph. I do know that at the time it doesn't feel that way, but know that it is.

Like Jacob, many of us know how it feels to be "left alone." When a love one dies or a friend leaves, or you walk through the fire of separation and divorce, no matter how "spiritual" you are it still hurts! Emotional pain to the soul what physical pain is to the body; it tells us that something is wrong; that we need God to guide us through the challenges and upheavals of realigning our life to cope with what has happened. And the struggle doesn't begin in earnest while we are surrounded by people, it starts when you are left alone. The fact is that we can survive without others, but we can't survive without God. That's why He sometimes strips away everything that make us dependent upon people. He sends certain individuals into our life to help build your faith and develop your character, and when they're gone, to leave you with the assurance that God's always in control.

The loss of loved ones (1) develops our spiritual muscle; (2) tests our resilience; (3) shows us the scope of God's power. When Moses died and Joshua was left in charge, God told him, "As I was with Moses, so I will be with thee." (Jos. 1:5). That's something that Joshua could have never learned while Moses was in the picture. And it's a lesson I learned after my husband was not in the picture. We must totally depend on God.

Many changes in our lives represent loss, whether as small as the cherished memory of a car or as large as a destroyed family home, a destroyed dream of success, or the death of a person we've deeply loved. In every loss we long for a touch of healing and hope. The book of Lamentations has been called "the funeral of a city."

In it, Jeremiah mourned the captivity of his people and the destruction of Jerusalem. Yet in the mist of sorrow there is a celebration of God's faithfulness: Through the Lord's mercies we are not consumed, because His compassions fail not. They are new every morning; great is Your faithfulness. "The Lord is my portion," says my soul, "therefore I hope in Him!" (Lam. 3:22-24). When our heart hurt because of loss, we can find hope in our Lord, who never changes.

While we are going through things in life, it is also a blessing to have true friendship with other believers. "As iron sharpens iron, so one man sharpens another." (Proverbs 27:17). Solid relationships keeps us grounded and accountable. I thank God that He placed some wonderful people in my life that has and still continues to help me stay grounded. I said earlier in my book that I didn't want to leave my church home in Boston because of the teaching and great fellowship. My Pastor and First Lady are true followers of God. They exhibit the true meaning of "servants of God." The first time we went to the church, they were having dinner for the congregation and they invited me and my husband to come downstairs and join them. We did, and at that time my husband wasn't saved; so he was quite reluctant. We sat down and immediately a member of the church said very rudely, "That's the Pastor and First Lady sit." My husband apologized and started to leave. The First Lady came up so humbly and said, "please take my sit." It is so important to show the love of God at all times because your behavior could be a deciding factor of whether that sinner accept Christ at that time. My husband felt so relieved and always talked about how humble the First Lady was.

Not only did we join the church, we became as family. And after my husband died I prayed that my pastor and his family would move to Atlanta. God released pastor (which is deceased now) and his wife presently live in Conyers, Georgia (praise God). God is so awesome! He will place significant people in your life, some who have the greatest influence in your life. Please remember that some relationships are only for a season and some are for a life time. I would like to take this time to name a few people that ministered with me over the years and that have such caring spirit. First and foremost is my dear mother Ruth; which is deceased, Carol Ann; my prayer partner, Cathy; my wonderful future daughter-in-law, Joanne; a long time dear friend, and last but not least.... Stephanie; my best friend for over twenty years and she has always shared my best interest. I love Stephanie for being the true friend that any person can ask for. My deceased husband had a best friend that I must also share with you and his name is Mr. Early Watkins. This man of

God taught us so much in Sunday School and amplifies that not only can you teach the Word but also live the Word. His famous quote that I will always remember is "If you fall for anything, you will stand for nothing." This man and these women of God have such a solid foundation in my life because they are those :

Slow to suspect, but quick to trust

Slow to condemn, but quick to justify

Slow to offend, but quick to defend

Slow to reprimand, but quick to forbear

Slow to belittle, but quick to appreciate

Slow to demand, but quick to forgive

These are some of the most influential people in my life that understood God's plan for my life that helped and did not try to hinder me. There maybe many friends that come and go in our lives but just know that Jesus is the only faultless friend that you will ever find.

God was so gracious that He placed me in a wonderful church home in Roswell, Georgia. I pray that people realize when they are under a leader that has a vision for the church that they need to catch a hold of the vision. I was so blessed to be a member of this church (for that season in my life) that have a young man that labor relentlessly for the Lord. He teaches the Word and has superb deacons. The time that my husband was going through therapy every deacon and the pastor took turns taking him to therapy. They expressed their love outside of the four walls. They were more than a blessing to me and I thank God for placing these wonderful men and women of God in my life. God's Word says "through love, let's serve one another---physically and spiritually--in the family of God (Gal. 5:13). They demonstrated that passage so well. No matter where God sends me, I will always be a part of Pleasant Hill Missionary Baptist Church. I am now under an awesome ministry at Open Door Outreach (Deliverance) Ministry under the supervision of a "dynamic" woman of God; which teaches and demonstrates the Word of God in her daily living. Again, thanks to the individuals above and to all that demonstrate the "love of God."

Trails can change our perspective on life. It is trite but true that how we deal with trials can make us bitter or better. In a remarkable statement , the psalmist actually thanked God for a difficult experience: "Before I was afflicted I went astray, but now I keep your Word..... It is good for me that I have been afflicted, that I may learn Your statures" (Ps. 119:67, 71). We don't know the nature of the psalmist's affliction, but the positive outcome was a longing to obey the Lord and a hunger for His Word. When we go through trials, it feels more like dying rather than growing. But as God wraps His loving arms around us, we have the assurance of His faithful care. We must learn to live by faith…not by feeling. Life is not always fair, but God is always faithful. Affliction for God's people can be the pruning knife to prepare us for greater fruitfulness. We can rest assure that when the sunshine of God's love meets the showers of our sorrow, the rainbow of promise appears. Life isn't about waiting for the storm to pass….It's about learning to dance in the rain.

You maybe going through a trial right now in your life, but know that prayer changes things and you can stand on the promises of God. Therefore I say unto you, what things soever ye desire, when ye pray, *believe* that ye receive them, and ye shall have them (Matt. 11:24). You might be going through a loss of a job, loss of a love one, imprisonment, drug addiction, alcohol addiction, a divorce, separation from family, back-biting, eviction, financial problems, disrespectful and disobedient children, betrayal of a friend, and so many trials, just to name a few. But whatever it may be, know that there is nothing too hard for God. Turn it over to Jesus and leave it there. You may say right now that "It isn't that simple." I am here to tell you " Yes it is!" God is the answer to all problems. And we as believers know that "All things work together for good to them that love God, to them who are called according to *His* purpose (Ro. 8:28). Not our purpose but His purpose.

God will always make good on His promises. God promised to send a Deliver who would forgive sin and restore the glory of Israel (Isa. 1:26, 53:12; 61). God had long ago promised one, but they hadn't heard a word from Him in 400 years. But then, at just the right moment, the angel announced to Joseph that Mary would give birth to a Son who would "save" His people from their sins" (Matt. 1:21). We know that God is a promise-keeping God! He said that He would send a Deliver, and He did. So your problems is not beyond reach. No matter how long you have been going through, God will be right on time to deliver you.

Trusting God can turn a crisis into a treasure. Crisis has a way of shaking us out of complacency. It reminds us this world is not our home and encourages us to focus on living for eternity. Our desire should be to live for Jesus whether circumstances are good or bad. We must learn to focus on His purpose. "Trust in the Lord with all thine heart; and lean not unto thine own understanding. In all thy ways acknowledge Him, and He shall direct our paths" (Proverbs 3: 5,6). God wants us to trust Him completely. Just like Noah, he trusted God even when it didn't make any sense. Trusting God means having faith that He knows what is best for our lives.

Remember the story of the aging Elizabeth who longed for a baby, and Mary, which pregnancy should have been a disgrace? But when both learned they would have a child, they accepted the news with faith in the God whose timing is perfect and whom nothing is impossible (Luke 1:24-25, 37-38). Their example shows us the value of a trusting heart that accepts the mysterious ways of God and the presence of His mighty hand, no matter how perplexing our circumstances may be. Sometimes we cannot see the outcome of a situation, we must learn to trust the Lord because He knows best. Just be assured He sees your trial, and He's with you throughout the test. As Christians we must learn that testing cannot be separated from trusting. When we trust the power of God we will always experience peace, not panic.

I remembered an incident years ago that occurred in my life that came to mind. I had a court date and was told by the judge that I needed to have this large sum of money by 2:00 P.M. that same day, or if not I would be arrested. In the natural, we would normally just panic trying to get the money, but instead of panicking I had such a peace. I trusted God and was led to go to noon day prayer at the church. As I entered the church I went and kneeled at the altar and just cried out to God. Not saying a word about my needs, but just trusting God. During prayer, my pastor called me and said open your hands and the Holy Spirit led her to instruct everyone to be a blessing to me. I received more than enough to pay the bill and had much more left over (praise God). I praised God for who He is and I thanked Him for what He did. It may not ever happen just like that for you but whichever way; the point is that if you trust God in every situation or circumstance, He is able to do all things but fail. "My God shall supply all your need according to His riches in glory by Christ Jesus (Philippians 4:19).

When we think of "blessings," the first thing comes to mind is a financial blessing. There is nothing wrong with being blessed financially, but know that God has many more blessings in store for us. It doesn't have to be a financial blessing for me to realize the "love of God." God is God all by Himself! I love Him because He first loved me. He is God! We must "Seek first the kingdom of God and His righteousness, and all these things shall be added to you" (Matt. 6:33). "Now unto him that is able to do exceeding abundantly above all that we ask or think, according to the power that worketh in us" (Ephesians 3:20).

Trusting comes along with obedience. Jesus said, "If you love me, you will keep my words; and my Father will love him, and we will come unto him, and make our abode with him (Jn. 14:23). That means that we must obey even when it doesn't seem to make any sense. We must learn to act without any hesitation or reluctance. "Behold, to obey is better than sacrifice, and to hearken than the fat of rams" (I Sam. 15:22). Obedience secures entrance into God's kingdom. "Not everyone that saith unto me, Lord, Lord, shall enter into the kingdom of heaven; but he that doeth the will of my Father which is in heaven (Mt. 7:21). We obey God because we love Him and trust that He knows what best for us. "It is better to trust in the Lord than to put confidence in man" (Ps. 118:8).

Going through is just what it says…going through. It isn't a permanent situation. We are passing through for that appointed time. This too shall pass because the Word says "Weeping may endure for a night, but joy, cometh in the morning" (Psalm 30:5). Your joy may be this very morning. "In the day of my trouble I will call upon You, for You will answer" (Psalm 86:7). Just call on the Lord and know that He will answer. Everyone has problems, but it's the inability to move beyond the problem, the inability to move pass the failures, that keep us in spiritual defeat. Victory is only found in the dependence of God.

Through all the storms, know that God will shelter you. In your hunger, God will feed you. Christians face struggles in today's world and it so easy to conform to worldly standards that we lose our identity as Christians without realizing it. We must ask ourselves, "How can I overcome the world and present a positive image of Jesus Christ?" Turn to God's Word which says, " For whatever is born of God overcomes the world; and this is the victory that has overcometh the world, even our faith" (1 John 5:4). Having faith in God is the key to overcoming the trials in our lives. "For we walk by faith, not by sight" (2 Co. 5:7). "Now faith is the substance of things hoped for, the evidence of things not seen" (He. 11:1). So then faith cometh by hearing, and hearing by the word of God (Ro. 10:17). Take the defending weapon. "Above all, taking the shield of faith, wherewith ye shall be able to quench all the fiery darts of the wicked" (1 Th. 5:8, Ti. 1:19, 6:12; He. 10:22). Hebrew 11:6 says "Without faith it is impossible to please him: for he that cometh to God must *believe* that he is, and that he is a rewarder of them that diligently seek him."

There are times in my life that I felt like a boxer and wanted to "throw in the towel" and just give up. The trials of life seem to weigh me down and was very heavy but I knew in my spirit that if I just hold on that it would get better. Like I said earlier that we are not exempt or immune from life trials, but we must learn to face them with the assurance that God is there to carry us through them. In the natural we want to "fix" things ourselves. Let me tell you when we try, we mess up every time! It was times in my life that I worried about everything. I would worry about worrying. Yes I did. Worry has never been a part of God's plan for man. Worry stems from our lack of trust in God. Thank God that I have been delivered from that "worrying spirit." I learned through that trial to cast all my cares, not just some; but all to Jesus because He cares for me.

My spiritual passion, at one point, had grown cold. I was just going through the motion. You know how we just go to church, just because we think that is the right thing to do? Well that was me. I had left my "first love." I began not to attend church as regular, didn't fellowship with the saints as much, didn't pray as I should, didn't read my Bible and certainly didn't walk in God's will. I was looking for love and compassion in all the wrong places. I was miserable. What can we do when something that energized us has become broken? Especially our relationship with Christ. I knew that I had to rediscover the passion that I longed for and missed. I cried out to recapture the fervor that always fueled me in the past......Jesus. The Word says, "Remember, therefore from where you have fallen, repent and do the first works" (Revelation 2:5). It is so easy to get side track and turn to "things," such as, our jobs, our children, our spouse, drugs, alcohol, relationships, friends and family. But I am here to tell you, that we need only to turn to our first love and that is…. Jesus. Jesus is bigger than any problem or circumstance we can face. Don't turn away from God, turn to God. We may look for all kinds of options, but…….Jesus is the only option that works.

When trouble comes into our lives, we sometimes feel as if we've been hit broadside. We tend to ask the question, "Why is this happening to me?" Ask yourself the question, "Why not me?" God maybe using that painful experience to get your attention and to lovingly persuade you to change. The season of trouble may not be easy, but if we let ourselves be trained by it, new growth will result as we become more like His Son (Phil. 3:10). "No chastening seems to be joyful for the present, but….it yields the peaceable fruit of righteousness to those who have been trained by it" (Hebrews 12:11). God does many things which we do not understand. Yes he does…He is God, perfect in wisdom, love and power. A true faith must rest solely on his character and his Word, not on our particular conceptions of what He ought to do.

I have been in the valley of despair, with disappointment after disappointment. I tried, like most of us, to figure things out by myself. I was looking to everyone and everything, but not depending totally on God.

Many times in our lives we feel that the small issues in life can be handled by ourselves but God wants us to cast [all] our cares on Him because He cares for us. Every incident that occurred in my life made me realized that I could not do anything without God. Every decision that we make we must consult the Great Consultant, which is....Jesus. Jesus says, take everything to Him in prayer. We make rash decisions in life that can produce lifelong consequences. We must never under-estimate the impact of our choices.

Joshua made a choice that we all can all follow. He told Israel, "Choose for yourselves this day whom you will serve," ..."But as for me and my house, we will serve the Lord" (Josh. 24:15). Serving God will not always be an easy choice but we can rest assure that it brings results that we can always live with. The results of what occurs in our lives tomorrow depends on the choices we make today.

I was living in a very small town in Georgia. I moved to this area because of a job opportunity. I could not understand at that point in my life , why I made the decision to take a job in a town that was so unfamiliar to what I was accustomed to. Many times in life, before receiving an answer from God, we react to what we think is best for us. I thought that this was the best for me at the time in my life. I arrived at the job and everything was going well. I stayed on the community where I worked and it gave me such a peace that I decided to relocate to this town. I would go to my room and just commune with God, in my quiet times. This is where I began to hear from God about returning to writing again.

As you know, no one is angry but the devil when God is moving in your life. Some of the employees began to turn against me with lies and jealousy. I endured that, but it ended in my termination. I know that all things work together for my good because what satan does to try and harm me God turned it around for my good. One of the same people that tried to hurt me was terminated shortly after me. God says in his Word, "Even the wrath of ungodly men praises to Him" (Ps. 76:10). You must be very careful about touching Gods' people. God will make your enemy your footstool. Romans 8:31 says, "If God be for us, who can be against us."

As I sat pondering on my financial status, about not having a job, God made me to know that He is my source. It was easy for me at this time in my life to sit and enjoy a pity party, because it was a trying time and it would have been easy for me just to feel sorry for myself. I could have blamed everyone for my failures or make every excuse at the time. Not having physical evidence of things can make a difference. But to know, even though I didn't have money to pay the bills, no job in sight, no friends or family to call on, I trusted God. We must learn to walk by faith and not by sight. No matter how it look I had to trust God. Everyday He supplied my needs. While going through, I remembered that, "You have been my defense and refuge in the day of trouble" (Ps. 59:16). No matter what our trouble is, God is right there. "Weeping may endure for a night, but joy, cometh in the morning."

In order to fulfill Gods' mission for our life, we must abandon our agenda and adopt Gods' plan for our lives. It begins by allowing Gods' will for our life. You must yield everything over to God and let go and let God. By saying and meaning within....not my will but your will. We must give ourselves completely to God, not just part but "all." When we completely commit our lives totally to God, we will experience the blessings of God in ways that you cannot imagine. There is nothing that God will not do for you if you commit to serving him. We must serve God in spirit and in truth. We must have faith to speak to those "mountains" in our lives to be removed. Whatever that mountain maybe, such as not having faith, not trusting, not believing when we don't see a way out of situations or circumstances or just not believing that with God "all" things are possible.

We are presently living in hard times of economic crisis, when our faith in God is so crucial. We must turn to God to get us through these times. In 2 Timothy 3:1-7 we are told that we are living in perilous times. As Christians we are not alarmed about the time we are experiencing at this time. We are not equipped to handle the problems we face, but know that God is. Sometimes in the midst of our trials, we need to think about the remarkable relationship we have with God through Jesus Christ. Jeremiah says in chapter 18 verse 7, " At what instant I shall speak concerning a nation, and concerning a kingdom, to pluck up, and to pull down and to destroy it." God is in control of everything. We must not worry about the times we are living in because God is calling us back to prayer. 2 Chronicles 7:14 says, "If my people, which are called by my name, shall humble themselves, and pray, and seek my face, and turn from their wicked ways; then will I hear from heaven, and I will forgive their sin, and heal their land."

In this life we tend to search for answers to worldly problems, such as, the stock market is looking for answers to correct the deficit, ways to end the war, the right president to lead the country, and financial crisis, just to name a few. Our answers is only ....Jesus. Trusting Jesus in troubled times (and all times) is the key. We cannot rely on man for the answer because we will surely fail.

took a trip to one of the most beautiful places in America. I visited Bermuda (which I must state, that this place is "the best kept secret) and was just overwhelmed. This small island is truly a breath-taking experience. As I arrived; thinking that I was going for a vacation and to surprise my sister, I was truly in for an ordeal of a life time! I arrived and just to see the exuberating colors of the houses, the pink sand on the beaches, was just breath-taking! But what was so awesome, was the peace of God that I felt as I entered this island. I have traveled many places in this world but I have never experienced the peace that I felt at this place. It was that peace that that made me see and feel the beauty of God! This trip was truly ordained by God. One of the most exciting things about this trip that will always stay dear to my heart was actually meeting a true woman of God.....Pastor Yvonne Ramsey. What an experience, just to be in the presence of a mighty warrior as this magnificent woman of God. I read her book and was truly blessed by the inspiring wisdom that God has given her. Gods' move was so awesome in the services that I attended and I seen the power of God in such a mighty way that I am still in awe. I sometime feel that I am still in Bermuda.

The wonderful blessings that I received; just being able to make this trip possible, was from a dear loving friend Ronita. I continually pray that God richly bless her in every area of her life. God has truly blessed her in the area of "giving" and she does it with such a loving spirit. The saints that inspired my life was a woman of God by the name of Valerie. She blessed me through songs of praise and a sand dollar necklace that will always be a remembrance of God love to me. There are so many treasures of Gods' blessings in this small island but I will always remember the peace that immersed my spirit and gave me a renewed walk with God.

My oldest son is engaged to be married, an entrepreneur and walking in his calling. My next oldest son is now getting his life together day by day. My youngest son is still incarcerated but saved and trusting God to release him any day now. My daughter is a nurse and have three beautiful children and resides in Boston. I have constant communication with all my wonderful grandchildren and great grand. I am now married to a wonderful man of God (Charles Williams); native of Jamaica, and he is such an inspiration to my life! He stands by my side and our love is wonderful. So believe me, there is nothing too hard for God!

As I conclude, I want you to remember to never get paralyzed by your past. Never let your pass dictate your future. Keep in your heart that the Word says, "For I know the plans I have for you, plans to prosper you and not to harm you, plans to give you hope and a future." You have a future in Christ! One of the great points in scripture is "perseverance." No matter how great your calling, your test or your trial, without perseverance you will give up. Remember the Word says, "blessed is the man that perseveres."

I returned back to Georgia with a renewed spirit. My oldest son is engaged to be married, an entrepreneur and walking in his calling. My next oldest son is now getting his life together day by day. My youngest son is still incarcerated but saved and trusting God to release him any day now. My daughter is a nurse and have three beautiful children and resides in Boston. I have constant communication with all my wonderful grandchildren and great grand. I am now married to a wonderful man of God (Charles Williams); native of Jamaica, and such an inspiration to my life! So believe me, there is nothing too hard for God!

Everyone goes through adversity but remember to just stay in that "dwelling place"; which is Jesus and you will find all the treasures that He has in store for you.

Thoughts to dwell on:

A person is just like a teabag,
You never know how strong they are until they are dipped
     in hot water.

You are my friend when you can guard my failure,
Challenge my thought and celebrate my success

Love looks beyond what people are
To what they become

You will keep your sanity
by keeping your faith

God often digs wells of joy
With the spade of sorrow

When God permits trials
He also provides comfort

What looks like a detour
May actually be a road to many blessings

Don't wait until the storm is over,
Dance in the rain

My Dwelling Place

When trials come to knock you down
Get back up and don't frown
Just stand tall in Jesus name
Victory, you can claim

No matter if it seem that the trial is long
Know that trials come to make us strong
Just stand tall in Jesus name
Victory, you can claim

No matter what may be the case
You have a dwelling place
Just stand tall in Jesus name
Victory, you can claim

A dwelling place in the most High
Allows God to hear every cry
Just stand tall in Jesus name
Victory, you can claim

My secret place gives me comfort to know
Jesus is differently the place to go
In time of trouble or despair
Go to my dwelling place
Jesus will be there
The One that really cares.

Printed in the United States
By Bookmasters